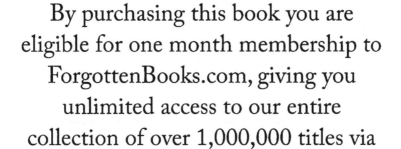

ISBN 978-0-265-92553-9
PIBN 10910770

st 4
5/14/13

U. S. DEPARTMENT OF AGRICULTURE.

BUREAU OF PLANT INDUSTRY—BULLETIN NO. 31.

B. T. GALLOWAY, Chief of Bureau.

CULTIVATED FORAGE CROPS

OF THE

NORTHWESTERN STATES.

BY

A. S. HITCHCOCK,

ASSISTANT AGROSTOLOGIST, IN CHARGE OF COOPERATIVE EXPERIMENTS,

GRASS AND FORAGE PLANT INVESTIGATIONS.

ISSUED DECEMBER 13, 1902.

WASHINGTON:

GOVERNMENT PRINTING OFFICE.

1902.

LETTER OF TRANSMITTAL.

U. S. DEPARTMENT OF AGRICULTURE,
BUREAU OF PLANT INDUSTRY,
OFFICE OF THE CHIEF,
Washington, D. C., October 17, 1902.

SIR: I have the honor to transmit herewith a paper on "Cultivated Forage Crops of the Northwestern States." and respectfully recommend that it be published as Bulletin No. 31 of the series of this Bureau.

This paper was prepared by Mr. A. S. Hitchcock, Assistant Agrostologist, in Charge of Cooperative Experiments, Grass and Forage Plant Investigations, and has been submitted with a view to publication by the Agrostologist.

Respectfully,

B. T. GALLOWAY,
Chief of Bureau.

Hon. JAMES WILSON,
Secretary of Agriculture.

PREFACE.

During the summer of 1901 Professor Hitchcock, under instructions from the then Agrostologist, Prof. F. Lamson-Scribner, visited the States of Kansas, Nebraska, Colorado, Wyoming, Utah, Nevada, California, Oregon, Washington, and Idaho for the purpose of studying conditions with reference to cultivated forage crops. In the course of his investigations he visited the experiment stations of the above States and interviewed many farmers and ranchmen, from some of whom he received much valuable information. Considerable information was also obtained from seedsmen and from dealers in grain and hay and farm machinery. The accompanying paper is a résumé of the information thus obtained. It is recognized that in a large section of country rather sparsely settled, and particularly one in which agriculture is a recent development, many farmers and others have learned much that would be valuable to others in the same section of country. The principal object of this paper is to make common property of the individual knowledge of various farmers, ranchmen, and others, so that each may benefit by the experience of others. This is particularly important in a new country such as the region described herein.

The paragraph relating to the "Inland Empire" and the last paragraph of the section devoted to velvet grass were written by the Agrostologist; otherwise the paper is entirely the work of Professor Hitchcock.

W. J. Spillman,
Agrostologist.

Office of the Agrostologist,
   Washington, D. C., October 14, 1902.

CONTENTS.

ILLUSTRATIONS.

                                8

CULTIVATED FORAGE CROPS OF THE NORTH-WESTERN STATES.

DESCRIPTION OF THE REGIONS.

The present bulletin discusses briefly the forage resources of that portion of the United States extending from Colorado and central California north to Montana and Washington. The whole area may be divided into several well-marked regions, each of which will be discussed separately. Each region has its characteristic climate, topography, and physiognomy. The climate depends chiefly upon the latitude, altitude, and the amount and distribution of the rainfall. The latter factor is greatly influenced by the presence and trend of the mountain chains and the direction of the prevailing winds. In general the winters are longer and more severe as the latitude increases. The climate is cooler at higher altitudes. The Coast Range, Sierra Nevada, and Cascade Mountains rob the winds of their moisture as they blow from the Pacific Ocean eastward, thus producing an arid region in the interior. The physiognomy, or general appearance, depends very largely upon the character of the vegetation, which in turn varies according to the climate and soil. The low and scattered vegetation of the sagebrush plains of the Great Basin region, the forests of the Pacific slope, and the buffalo-grass sod of the Great Plains are examples of the characteristic physiognomy. It is not the intention to discuss minutely the physical geography of the region, but these preliminary remarks will call attention to the basis of the regional classification. The relation of these physical factors to the agriculture of the individual regions will be referred to later.

The soil conditions are more local in their effect than the above-mentioned factors, but in some cases may profoundly modify the growth of plants. The soil factors may be physical, such as its ability to hold or transport water, the size of the particles, and character of the subsoil; or chemical, depending upon the chemical constituents, such as the presence of excessive amounts of carbonate of soda, salt, or other substances, producing alkali soils. One other factor should be mentioned, which, though not included among those determining the classification into areas, is nevertheless of vast importance in its relation to agriculture. This is artificial water supply or irrigation.

GREAT PLAINS.

This region extends from about the ninety-eighth meridian to the Rocky Mountains and from Texas far north into Canada. The altitude increases from about 1,500 feet, at the eastern limit, to the base of the mountains, where it may be 6,000 or 7,000 feet. The western portion of this area extends into the group of States considered in this bulletin. The topographical features of this region are discussed by the late Thomas A. Williams in Bulletin No. 12 of the Division of Agrostology, U. S. Department of Agriculture, entitled "A Report upon the Grasses and Forage Plants and Forage Conditions of the Eastern Rocky Mountain Region."

The annual rainfall is usually from 10 to 12 inches, in consequence of which the cultivation of crops is dependent upon irrigation. The native grasses are well adapted to grazing, and hence stock raising is the paramount industry throughout this portion of the Great Plains, which includes the eastern part of the States of Montana, Wyoming, and Colorado. The stock raised is chiefly cattle and sheep, vast herds of which roam over the plains during the summer, and, in most localities, for the greater part of the winter, subsisting upon the short grasses, the most important of which are buffalo grass (*Bulbilis dactyloides*) and blue grama (*Bouteloua oligostachya*). Along the draws or in the valleys of the streams taller grasses occur, such as blue-stem (*Andropogon furcatus*) and alkali saccaton (*Sporobolus airoides*), the common bunch grass of the Arkansas Valley. The upland or "short" grasses seldom grow sufficiently tall for hay, but in favorable seasons hay is cut in those situations where the tall grasses abound. The foliage of the short grasses usually cures on the ground and furnishes food through the winter; but in order to provide food during the stormy periods of the winter and to increase the carrying capacity of the ranges by supplementing the natural food supply, hay is put up for winter use. This practice is increasing as competition enforces more economical methods of agriculture. Almost all the forage stored for winter is produced by the aid of irrigation. Near the base of the mountains there is an abundant supply of water in the mountain streams, and this is distributed along the valleys by means of canals. In many places storage reservoirs supply water in the canals during a portion of the period of low water.

The most important forage plant raised by cultivation is alfalfa. This can be grown up to an elevation of 5,000 or 6,000 feet. On account of the altitude the nights are too cold for the successful cultivation of corn and many other of the coarse forage grasses grown in the prairie regions to the east. Sorghum and Kafir corn are grown to some extent in Colorado for forage. Timothy is grown, especially in the mountain region; it is used for both pasture and hay. Red clover is raised in Montana and to some extent in the two States to the south. The recently introduced awnless brome grass has shown that it can be successfully grown without irrigation. For a further discussion of the forage conditions of this area the reader is referred to Bulletin No. 12 mentioned above.

ROCKY MOUNTAIN REGION.

This includes a wide area passing through Colorado, Wyoming, western Montana, and a part of eastern Idaho. This area also received attention in Bulletin No. 12.

As in the preceding area, the most important agricultural industry is stock raising. Sheep raising is relatively more important here. The sheep are pastured during the summer in the valleys, or at least where they have access to water, but during the winter they may be driven to the more arid districts, depending upon the snowfall for their water supply.

The forage conditions of one of these arid regions is discussed by Prof. Aven Nelson in Bulletin No. 13 of the Division of Agrostology, U. S. Department of Agriculture, entitled "The Red Desert of Wyoming and its Forage Resources."

Alfalfa is raised by irrigation at the lower altitudes throughout the area, but, as before stated, is not successful at an altitude exceeding 6,000 or 7,000 feet, depending upon the latitude, and somewhat upon the local conditions. Above this altitude the common forage grasses of the East may be grown. Timothy is raised in Colorado in favorable locations up to an elevation of 9,000 or even 10,000 feet. On the plateau from Laramie westward the ranchmen depend largely upon wild hay for winter food. This is irrigated to increase the crop; but, owing to the injudicious or excessive application of water, the more desirable grasses are driven out by "wire grass" (*Juncus balticus*), a kind of rush.

It is a common practice to flood the land in the spring and allow it to remain partly under water until time for cutting the hay, when the water is turned off. A species of spike rush (*Eleocharis*), also known as wire grass, is common in the moist spots. This wire grass is only moderately nutritious, but yields larger crops of hay than when grown on unirrigated land, and it is less trouble to turn on the water once than to supply the water oftener, allowing it to drain off each time.

There is an impression among farmers in southern Wyoming that wild hay is more valuable for feed than alfalfa, ton for ton, for all kinds of stock. This is reflected in the price of hay at Saratoga, where wild hay or timothy sold at $15 and alfalfa at $5 to $6 per ton. At Laramie baled native hay was worth $8 to $10, and alfalfa in the stack $5 to $7 per ton. Throughout the West, grass hay is considered better than alfalfa for horses. There are several other kinds of forage plants that have been grown in isolated localities with success, and whose cultivation should be extended. Among these may be mentioned the Canada field pea, rape, and awnless brome grass.

GREAT BASIN.

This region extends from the Sierra Nevada Mountains to the Rocky Mountains, and from Arizona north into southeastern Oregon and southern Idaho. It is an arid region, having an annual rainfall of less than 15 inches over the greater part, and in central Nevada of less than 5 inches. The altitude of this great plateau is about 5,000 or 6,000 feet, with numerous mountain chains rising 2,000 or 3,000 feet higher. There are several lakes or depressions having no outlet, the largest of which is the Great Salt Lake of Utah.

In such localities there is usually an excessive accumulation of mineral salts, known as alkali. The water of the streams flowing into these depressions holds these salts in solution, but deposits them upon the surface of the soil when the water evaporates. These alkali soils modify the vegetation. Each species of plant is able to withstand a certain amount of alkali in the soil upon which it grows. If the amount is in excess of this limit, the plant can not exist. Consequently, the native vegetation gives a fair index of the alkaline condition of the soil. The presence of saltbushes (*Atriplex* spp.), salt grass (*Distichlis spicata*), and grease wood (*Sarcobatus vermiculatus*) indicates a strongly alkaline soil. A still larger amount of soluble mineral matter prevents the growth of even the salt plants, and in such cases the soil is devoid of vegetation.

The prevailing vegetation over the whole region, except in the mountains and upon the above-mentioned alkali soils, is the sagebrush (*Artemisia tridentata*). Hence such localities are called sagebrush plains. As in the case of the two preceding areas the chief agricultural industry is the raising of stock—cattle, sheep, and horses. The latter class of stock is of importance in certain localities, but is relatively unimportant over the whole area. The sheep are herded in the mountains in summer, where there is water, and upon the deserts in winter, where there is snow. There are vast areas where stock can not graze on account of the insufficiency of food or water, or both.

Alfalfa is grown in large quantities under irrigation in the valleys and is practically the only supplemental forage for all kinds of stock. In some of the larger valleys other crops are raised, such as grain and sugar beets. As an example, the highly cultivated Cache Valley, in northern Utah, may be mentioned. In a few favored localities dry farming may be carried on successfully. This, however, is where there is seepage and conservation of water from the winter snow on the mountains. In the Cache Valley there are numerous instances of grain and alfalfa fields on the hillsides above the canals.

INTERIOR VALLEY OF CALIFORNIA.

Between the Coast Range and the Sierra Nevada Mountains lies a valley extending through central California from Kern County on the south to Shasta County on the north. This is formed by the union of two valleys, the Sacramento River flowing from the north and the San Joaquin from the south. The region is characterized by high temperature and scant rainfall in the summer. The Coast Range Mountains forming the western limit of the valley cut off the moisture-laden winds from the Pacific Ocean, except at San Francisco Bay, where there is a break in the chain through which the above-mentioned rivers reach the ocean. At this point in the valley and also opposite a few other minor breaks, the climate is modified in proportion to the amount of moisture that filters through.

When the winter rainfall is sufficient there may be an abundance of native pasture during the spring, but the main dependence is placed on two crops—alfalfa and grain hay. Excepting in a few favored localities, crops are raised by the aid of irrigation. The alfalfa is mostly consumed upon the farm, while the grain· hay supplies the city markets. Alfalfa grows to the greatest perfection, especially in the San Joaquin Valley, where it is customary to obtain about 8 tons of hay at five cuttings from each acre, and about five months' pasture. Grain hay is produced from wheat, barley, and, to a less extent. from oats. In some districts, wild-oat hay is common.

UPPER PACIFIC COAST REGION.

This includes the area lying along the coast west of the Cascade Mountains, from Puget Sound south to San Francisco. It is characterized by cool summers, mild winters, and a large rainfall. Fogs are frequent and droughts very rare. The conditions are very favorable for the growth of pasture grasses, and the section is preeminently a dairy region. Through most of this region cattle can be pastured through the winter. Some hay is preserved, especially in western Washington, but on account of the dampness the quality is inferior. The Willamette Valley of western Oregon may be considered as a part of this general area, though, since it is shut off from the coast by a low range of mountains (the Coast Range), the rainfall is much less, and the climate is correspondingly modified. The annual rainfall here is 40 to 60 inches, mostly in the winter. Along the coast the rainfall is 60 inches, increasing northward in the region of Puget Sound, and it is distributed throughout most of the year. In this region the grasses and clovers that are commonly used in the Eastern States grow in great luxuriance.

THE "INLAND EMPIRE."

This region, sometimes known as the Palouse country, comprises eastern Washington, northeastern Oregon, and northern Idaho. It is characterized by a dark, fine-grained basaltic soil of great fertility and of very uniform character over a wide area. The limiting factors of agriculture here are rainfall and altitude. With Pasco, Wash., as a center, where the annual rainfall is about 6 inches, the rainfall increases in all directions, attaining a maximum of about 30 inches at the base of the Blue and Rocky mountains on the east, and the Cascade Mountains on the west. A considerable portion of this area in Washington and a smaller section in Oregon have a rainfall of less than 10 inches. In this portion irrigation is practiced. In Washington, about 150,000 acres are under irrigation within this area, alfalfa being the staple hay crop, with a yield of 3 to 8 tons of hay per acre, at three cuttings. The principal irrigated areas are situated in Yakima, Kittitas, Walla Walla, and Chelan counties, Wash. Smaller areas, especially in narrow canyons along the smaller streams, are located in various parts of Oregon and Washington. The Kittitas Valley in Washington, which lies at a higher altitude (about 1,600 feet) than any other considerable irrigated area in the region in question, grows alfalfa, timothy, and clover, producing hay of excellent quality. Like all other regions between the Cascades and the Rockies, the haying season is free from rain, which fact accounts for the excellent quality of hay produced.

Those portions of the "Inland Empire" having more than 10 inches of rainfall have heretofore been devoted almost exclusively to wheat growing. In recent years considerable attention has been given to hay and pasture grasses. Brome grass (*Bromus inermis* L.) has proven to be an excellent pasture grass in this region. It also yields profitable crops of hay the second and third years after sowing. A superior quality of brome grass seed is produced here. Of the hay grasses, timothy and red clover are preferred for lowlands and alfalfa, red clover, and orchard grass for uplands. On these wheat lands, which lie at an altitude of 1,500 to 3,000 feet, alfalfa produces one or two crops a year, and is rapidly becoming an important hay crop. Irrigation is not practiced in this region where the rainfall exceeds 10 or 12 inches a year.

Heretofore, and even at the present time, the principal hay of the wheat-growing area has been a mixture of wheat and wild oats (*Avena fatua*). Where the rainfall exceeds 18 inches wild oats are troublesome in the wheat fields, particularly on north hillsides, where snow banks protect them against freezing. Hay is cut from those patches in the wheat fields where wild oats predominate. When cut green this hay is of good quality, but many careless farmers cut it so late that the seeds are mature, and the hay is not only of poor quality but serves to scatter the seed of the pest. The common system of farming consists of taking a crop of wheat every alternate year, leaving the land idle every other year. During the idle year the land is summer fallowed: that is, plowed up in spring and left bare during summer. These fallow fields often furnish excellent wild-oat pastures, which are generally utilized.

At the present time alfalfa, clover, and brome hay are beginning to take the place of grain hay in this wheat-growing section. It has been learned that an exhausted brome-grass field can be restored to its early vigor by plowing in winter and harrowing to good tilth. After this plowing, a crop of spring grain may be taken without serious injury to the brome grass.

FORAGE CROPS.

ALFALFA[a] (*Medicago sativa*).

GENERAL CONDITIONS.

This well-known forage plant is extensively grown throughout the West in all localities where the conditions are suitable. It requires a well-drained soil and a fairly good supply of water, but will not endure an excess of water (standing water) near the surface. It thrives best where the summers are hot and dry and the winters not too cold. It will withstand a moderate amount of alkali in the soil. In the North it suffers in some localities from the effects of too cold winters, and is not usually successful above an altitude of 5,000 or 6,000 feet. It can be grown without irrigation in but comparatively few localities in the Northwest; but under irrigation it is extensively grown in all the States of this region, and reaches its greatest perfection in the hot, dry valleys of California, where the summer season is long, the water supply abundant, and the soil well drained. Alfalfa will not succeed on acid soils, but these are of rare occurrence in the western part of the United States.

Alfalfa is a perennial leguminous plant, a native of western Asia, but cultivated in the Old World for ages. It was brought to Mexico by the Spaniards and from there spread into South America and north along the Pacific coast, and then throughout the interior arid and semiarid regions. The name alfalfa, of Arabic origin, was given by the Spaniards and is in common use throughout western America. In Europe the same plant is known as lucern, a name which is common in the eastern United States, and also in Utah and the adjacent parts of Idaho and Wyoming. In the latter region the name is commonly pronounced with the accent on the first syllable.

---

[a] For further description see Farmers' Bulletin No. 31.

Being a legume, it gathers nitrogen from the air by means of its root nodules, and hence acts as a soil renovator. Although alfalfa is a perennial, a field usually deteriorates after a few years from various causes. Fields in California as much as 27 and in Nevada from 35 to 40 years old are reported, but in most cases they require renewing much earlier. Often the alfalfa fields become infested with weeds. The squirrel-tail grass (*Hordeum jubatum*)—also called foxtail in Wyoming, barley grass in Utah, and tickle grass in Nevada—is common in alfalfa fields of the Great Basin and Wyoming plateau region, and wild barley (*Hordeum murinum*)—also called barley grass and fox-tail—on the Pacific slope.

These two grasses are especially troublesome on account of the long bristles attached to the chaff. When mature they cause serious irritation in the mouths of animals eating hay containing the weed. In the Cache Valley and in western Wyoming the common dandelion is very troublesome. It thrives along irrigation ditches and invades the alfalfa fields to such an extent that usually the fields are plowed up in from five to eight years and renewed. This is done in the fall and oats are sown the following spring, after which the fields are again seeded down to alfalfa.

Many express the opinion that under favorable conditions an alfalfa field will last indefinitely and continue to yield profitable crops if properly handled; but the alfalfa may be killed in spots due to the trampling of stock if a field is overpastured, or, during irrigation, certain portions of the field being lower, may remain saturated with water for too long a period. Alfalfa will scarcely survive standing water longer than forty-eight hours. When alfalfa dies, its place is likely to be taken by the before-mentioned pernicious weeds.

Some growers renew their fields by disking the bare spots in the spring and sowing seed thereon, or even disking the whole field. Disking is to be recommended, as it cuts the crowns vertically and causes them to send out new stems.

FEEDING VALUE.

In the great alfalfa districts of the West this forage plant furnishes the chief and often the only food for stock besides the native pasture. It is fed to growing stock and to fattening stock; to cattle, sheep, horses, and hogs; even the work horses upon the ranches may receive no grain in addition to the allowance of alfalfa. Horses that are worked hard upon the road, such as livery teams, usually receive a small quantity of barley, and this grain may form a part of the ration for the work horses upon the ranches. Rolled barley is the form in which it is usually fed, as in this condition there is said to be less waste than when whole or ground. For this purpose the grain is passed through heavy rollers, which crush it without grinding it.

There is much difference of opinion among farmers as to the value of alfalfa for horses. Some prefer timothy or wild hay, together with grain; some feed alfalfa and grain, while others maintain that horses do well enough upon alfalfa alone. It is usually admitted that for hard work, horses should be given at least a small allowance of grain.

In Wyoming some ranchmen claim that wild hay gives a firmer flesh than alfalfa, and thus, even when feeding the latter to cattle being prepared for the market, the stockmen will feed wild hay for about two weeks prior to shipment. Some feeders finish by adding grain to the ration. For this purpose barley is used, as it is the only grain available through most of the Northwest. The seasons are too short or the nights too cold for the successful cultivation of corn, the standard feeding grain of the region to the east, and freight rates make this grain when shipped too expensive for use. At Fort Collins and adjacent parts of Colorado large numbers of sheep are fattened for the market upon alfalfa and corn. It is said that about 300,000 were fed in that vicinity during the winter of 1900–1901. Lambs weighing 35 or 40 pounds are brought from the ranges of New Mexico and fed from about the 1st of October until sold, which may be anywhere from February to June. The yearlings will then weigh from 70 to 90 pounds.

It is stated[a] "that 40 acres of alfalfa will keep 300 sheep when pastured upon it. There is danger of bloating at first, but as soon as the sheep have become accustomed to it this danger ceases. Forty acres of alfalfa and 20 acres of grain will feed 450 to 500 head."

In many parts of the Great Basin it is customary for feeders to buy alfalfa in the stack for winter feeding, paying a certain amount per head per day. Conveniences for weighing are usually lacking, and this method seems to be satisfactory. At Lovelocks, which lies in one of the great alfalfa districts of central Nevada, the price for cattle was 7 to 8 cents per head and for sheep 1 cent per head per day. In Nevada, and also in some other districts of the Northwest, the stock cattle are kept upon the range during the winter, though the ranchmen try to provide a supply of alfalfa or wild hay for use during snowstorms. A selection is made from the herd, however, of those that are to receive winter feed with more regularity. These are the weaklings, the heifers with calf, and the cows with calves by their sides. It is also customary to feed only the old or weak sheep during the winter, the remainder being turned upon the deserts for their winter range.

Some common forms of racks for feeding alfalfa to cattle and sheep are shown in Pls. V and VI.

Though some maintain that grain hay is better for feeding cattle, ton for ton, than alfalfa, the majority of feeders state that the reverse has been their experience. Mr. G. F. Chapman, of Evanston, Wyo., states

[a] Agricola Aridus, published by the Colorado Agricultural College, I, p. 24.

9495—No. 31—02——2

that he has many times tried to raise cows with calves upon wild hay, but that the calves often die of starvation, while when fed upon alfalfa both cow and calf remain in good condition.

SEEDING.

The soil should be well prepared and finely pulverized, as the young alfalfa is a tender plant. In those localities where the rainfall is depended upon for the water supply, the seed should not be sown until a rain has moistened the soil thoroughly and thus placed it in a condition to favor germination. In California the rains come with such regularity that the seed may often be sown in advance of a rain and thus get the full benefit of the favorable conditions.

The seed is sown in the spring, except in central California, where it may be sown in either fall or spring. In California a common method is to irrigate, if necessary, in September or October, prepare the soil, and then to sow the seed broadcast with barley, or sometimes wheat. There is some danger from frost, and the grain is thought to protect the alfalfa. It is best not to pasture the alfalfa the first season, but to allow it to obtain a good start for the second season. If sown in the spring, the grain is usually omitted.

In other parts of the Northwest, alfalfa, though sown in the spring, is sown either alone or with grain—barley, wheat, or oats. Mr. W. P. Noble, of Golconda, Nev., states that alfalfa is sometimes sown with timothy in central Nevada. Sowing with grain has the advantage that there is a return from the land the first season, while the alfalfa is getting started. When sown with grain it is best not to pasture the alfalfa or cut it for hay the first season. After harvesting the grain, the alfalfa should be irrigated, and for this reason the grain should be removed from the field as soon as possible.

On the other hand, many prefer to sow the alfalfa alone, as in this way a better stand is obtained. Under favorable conditions one cutting may be obtained the first season, but it is not best to draw too heavily upon the field the first year either by cutting or pasturing the crop. Where the ground is weedy, it may be necessary to cut the weeds in the summer; but a still better plan is to previously free the soil from weeds by proper methods of cultivation.

When alfalfa is sown with grain, the two may be sown at the same time by means of combination machines which drill the grain and alfalfa through the same holes or scatter the alfalfa broadcast in front of the grain drill, or the alfalfa may be drilled one way and the grain cross-drilled, or the two may be sown broadcast and harrowed in separately. The amount of seed recommended by alfalfa growers varies from 12 to 30 pounds per acre. When the seed is drilled in, the amount required is less than when sown broadcast. The larger quantities of seed tend to produce smaller stems and the hay contains less waste. Under average conditions 20 pounds per acre sown broadcast should be sufficient. if it is evenly distributed and covered to a uniform depth: but a few pounds more per acre may be sown to insure a good stand. Where alfalfa is grown for a crop of seed. a less quantity should be sown than where a permanent meadow is desired.

MAKING HAY.

As stated. it is best not to cut a crop of alfalfa hay the first season, but to allow the field to get well started for the next year. However, under favorable conditions. especially in California. one or even two or three crops of hay may be obtained the first year. The grower must use his judgment as to whether a crop can be taken from the field to advantage. In California it is customary to make two cuttings if the seed was sown in the fall with grain: the first cutting consists mostly of grain. and the second of alfalfa. After the first year the number of cuttings depends upon the length of the season and the altitude. At the higher altitudes or latitudes not more than two cuttings may be possible. while in the upper San Joaquin Valley in California five or six cuttings are usually obtained. and as high as ten cuttings are reported. The fields are usually irrigated once for each cutting, either before or after. If the irrigation is made after the cutting, sufficient time should elapse to allow the growth to commence. or there is danger of scalding. At Newman. which is in the center of the alfalfa district of the San Joaquin Valley. the first cutting is made about May 1, and others at intervals of four to eight weeks. six weeks being about the average. The last cutting is made in September. after which. for about four months, the fields are pastured. The yield of hay here for the season is about 8 tons per acre. though some farmers state that only three or four cuttings were made, yielding 5 tons. The opinion was expressed that the fields were often pastured too much. On the high plains of southern Wyoming only two cuttings are usually made. yielding about 5 tons of hay per acre. In the Lovelock Valley. Nev.. where large quantities of alfalfa are grown. three cuttings are made, with a yield of 5 to 7 tons.

Alfalfa hay is prepared in the manner usual for hay crops, but the operations are modified somewhat by the climatic conditions prevailing in the dry regions of the Northwest. One man with a team can mow about 15 acres per day. The alfalfa is usually raked within a few hours after mowing, thrown into bunches by hand, and stacked as soon as convenient. If the hay is allowed to remain too long in the swath or windrow, too much loss of foliage occurs in stacking on account of the dryness of the air. The stacks may be put up in the field or near the corrals, according to convenience. If the fields are pastured during the latter part of the year, the stacks are inclosed by a fence. In some sections, especially in California, where there are winter rains, the hay is often stored in barns or sheds.

The hay is usually stacked by machinery. If the stack is made in the field, sweeps or bull rakes are occasionally used for hauling the bunches to the stacks, but these implements have the serious objection of shattering the leaves, causing corresponding loss of valuable fodder. For this reason the bunches are usually loaded by hand on wagons provided with hay racks (Pl. IV, fig. 1). At the stack the hay is unloaded from the wagons by horsepower, the machine used for this purpose being called a stacker or hay derrick.

The most common type of stacker throughout the Northwest is some modification of the pole, or mast and boom, stacker. This is essentially a derrick, with pulleys and a hay fork, by which several hundred pounds of hay can be lifted from a wagon and deposited upon the stack. Pl. II, Pl. III, and Pl. IV, fig. 2, show some of these forms. The stackers are generally homemade. The derrick may be supported by a heavy framework or may consist of poles held in place by guy ropes. The hay is usually lifted by means of a fork, but nets are in common use in some localities. The most common style of fork is that known as the Jackson fork, or, outside of California, as the California fork. For alfalfa the fork usually has four tines, but for grass hay five or six tines. By means of a small rope the operator upon the wagon can dump the fork load of hay upon the stack at any desired point. (See Pl. I, fig. 1.) One or two horses attached to the lifting rope or cable furnish the power to lift the load. The load on the fork is swung over the stack by slightly leaning the derrick toward the stack. The fork then swings by its own weight. The empty fork is drawn back to the wagon by means of the dump rope. Sometimes the load is swung over the stack by hand. Another form of fork occasionally seen is the harpoon fork. Instead of the fork there is sometimes used a net, also called a sling or hammock. Three or four of these are placed at intervals in the hay as it is being loaded. At the stacks, the nets full of hay are lifted from the wagon to the stack by means of derricks.

Another form of stacker which has proven very satisfactory is the cable derrick. Pl. I, fig. 2, illustrates this form. Forks or nets may be used with this style. In eastern Colorado and parts of Wyoming an improved stacker was in common use.

The bunches may be brought to the stacker with horse sweeps, but the distance must not be great or there will be too much loss of leaves. Hence the stacks are smaller than when the bunches are brought by wagon.

The stacks of alfalfa are commonly made about 25 feet wide and high, and as long as convenient, often 100 or more feet.

Throughout most of the alfalfa region the hay is put up during the dry season, and the process can therefore go on without fear of interruption from showers. Hence no pains are taken to top off the stack in order to shed rain until the stack is finished.

TURKESTAN ALFALFA.

Turkestan alfalfa, a variety recently introduced from Russian Turkestan by the U. S. Department of Agriculture, has been tried in many parts of the Northwest, but over most of this region it appears to have no superiority over the kind already grown. Experiments seem to show, however, that it is somewhat more resistant to cold than the common variety: hence it is likely to be better adapted to the colder portions of the area, such as Washington, Oregon, and Idaho.

TIMOTHY (*Phleum pratense*).

This standard grass is extensively grown in many parts of the Northwest, particularly where the climate is too moist and cool for alfalfa, such as the mountain districts and the Pacific coast plain west of the Coast Range. It is the most commonly cultivated grass in the Rocky Mountain region, thriving in the higher altitudes where alfalfa is not successful. Except in favored locations, the fields must be irrigated. Timothy will not usually succeed in the hot, dry valleys of California and the southern portion of the Great Basin region, even when irrigated. In the irrigated regions of central Washington, timothy is an important crop, being grown chiefly above 1,200 feet altitude. The Ellensburg district of the Yakima Valley is famous for the excellent quality and large quantity of timothy grown for shipment. On account of the dryness of the air the hay retains its fresh green color, while that grown in the very moist regions around Puget Sound and along the coast to the southward is usually darker colored. For this reason there is a strong demand for timothy grown in the irrigated districts around Ellensburg, Wash., and elsewhere in northeastern Washington and in northern Idaho, for export. As stated in another chapter, this timothy is baled in large quantities for the Alaskan and Philippine markets by the process of double compression. Where grown for home consumption, timothy is often mixed with red clover. The timothy may be sown in the fall and the clover in the spring, with oats; or the oats may be sown in the spring and the other two mixed and sown broadcast later. Sometimes the clover and timothy are sown together by means of combination drills. These machines have a separate feed box for the clover, which may drop the seed in the same holes with the timothy or sow it broadcast in front of the drill. On moister land and certain kinds of gravelly soil, alsike replaces the red clover in combination with timothy.

Timothy, either alone or in combination with clover, is frequently used for pasture. The method of establishing pasture employed by Mr. Wheeler, who owns a ranch near Reno, Nev., illustrates the possibilities in this direction, where water is available. Upon ordinary sagebrush land, and without previous preparation, a mixture of alfalfa, timothy, red clover, and orchard grass were sown. Beyond irrigation, nothing further was done. The pasture, now 3 years old, is in excellent condition and consists chiefly of alfalfa and timothy. Under this treatment the sagebrush has gradually disappeared, though the dead stems may be found on the ground beneath the growth of grass. A meadow can be established in the same manner, but it is then necessary to level the land by some means, such as dragging the surface with heavy railroad iron drawn by several horses.

Grain Hay.

In central California and parts of the interior region, hay made from cereals is an important product. Grain hay is made from wheat, which is considered the best; from barley, and, to a less extent, from oats, though in many localities wild oat hay is commonly preserved. As previously stated, alfalfa is generally consumed on the farm, while grain hay supplies the city markets. For convenience it is usually baled. It is often the case that the price of the grain determines whether the crop shall be converted into hay or the grain be allowed to mature. For hay, the grain is cut when between the milk and the dough stages. It is preserved the same as other hay, but is allowed to cure in the bunch. It may then be stacked or, if possible, baled from the bunch. As there is little or no rain in the grain-hay region of California, there is little danger of injury from this cause by leaving the hay in the bunches.

On a large ranch near Lovelocks, Nev., an example was presented of the use of wheat to supplement the alfalfa crop. The latter had been seriously injured by the ravages of a variety of field mouse. Wheat was sown in the spring to fill up the places left bare from this cause and the mixed crop was converted into hay in the usual manner.

Redtop (*Agrostis alba*).

Redtop is frequently grown on wet meadows in the northern Rocky Mountain region and to some extent in other localities. It is not considered as valuable a grass as timothy, but from the fact that it thrives in moist land and can be sown upon native meadow, where under irrigation it resists fairly well the encroachments of rushes (wire grass), it is utilized both for hay and pasture. It is not usually grown alone, but with other grasses or clovers.

Awnless Brome Grass (*Bromus inermis*).

Awnless brome grass [a] has been grown for many years in Europe,

---

[a] For further information concerning this grass, see Circular No. 18, Division of Agrostology, U. S. Dept. of Agriculture, "Smooth Brome Grass."

where it is native. In recent years it has been tried in many parts of the United States with varying degrees of success. It has proven most successful in the semiarid regions of the Northwest from Kansas and North Dakota to Washington. It is especially adapted for those regions where the rainfall is insufficient to grow forage crops without irrigation and yet the conditions do not approach the aridity of the desert. Such regions are found in the eastern part of the Great Plains, plateaus in the Rocky Mountains, and the Palouse region of eastern Washington.

The seed may be sown broadcast in the spring, at the rate of about 20 pounds to the acre. The stand is usually thin the first year, but the second year it thickens up and forms a sod. In localities where winter wheat can be grown, brome grass can be sown in the fall. It is valuable for hay, but more especially for pasture. During midsummer the foliage dries up more or less, but gives good pasture in early spring and late fall. The second year it yields large crops of palatable hay, but thereafter it is better adapted for pasture than for hay. (See Pl. VII, fig. 2.)

Velvet Grass (*Holcus lanatus*).

This grass is common in the Pacific coast region along roadsides, in abandoned fields and other waste places, and also is found encroaching upon pasture land. It is a native of Europe, but has been introduced into many parts of the United States. Opinions differ as to its usefulness, some stigmatizing it as a vile weed, others referring to it as a valuable forage grass. It is not a very large yielder, but will thrive on poor soil where more valuable grasses fail. Hence in localities where the usual meadow and pasture grasses flourish the advent of velvet grass should be looked upon with disfavor, but on more sterile soil it furnishes a fair crop of forage where other grasses fail. It has been said that "velvet grass is a good grass for poor land, and a poor grass for good land." Velvet grass goes under the name of mesquite in many parts of the Northwest, but this name is more frequently applied to certain native grasses of the Southwest.

On sandy soils along the coast and on peaty soils that dry out in summer, velvet grass is perhaps the most profitable hay and pasture grass, because the better grasses do not succeed. Stock usually refuse to eat it at first until driven to do so by hunger, but they will soon acquire a taste for it, and it is exceedingly nutritious. Its worst faults are its low yield and lack of palatability.

Clovers.

Red clover (*Trifolium pratense*) is in common cultivation throughout the northern portion of the Rocky Mountain and upper Pacific coast regions and is rapidly coming into cultivation in the more moist parts of eastern Washington and northern Idaho. Two crops of hay may be obtained, although in western Washington the approach of the rainy season may interfere with the second crop. The seed is usually sown in the spring, but on sandy land in western Washington it may be sown in the fall. As mentioned under the head of timothy, red clover is usually sown in combination with that plant.

Alsike clover (*T. hybridum*) is occasionally grown in the same localities where red clover thrives, but it is adapted to more moist land.

White clover (*T. repens*) is sometimes cultivated in combination with bluegrass in those localities where the latter thrives. Such pastures are frequently found in the mountain districts and along the upper coast region.

FORAGE CROPS OF MINOR IMPORTANCE.

The following forage plants are cultivated in sufficient abundance to receive attention. Some are already of importance in certain localities, and most of them should be cultivated over a wider area and given greater attention than is now the case:

KENTUCKY BLUEGRASS (*Poa pratensis*).—In the mountain districts and the upper coast region bluegrass is used for pasture, usually in combination with white clover. Unless supplied with water during the summer months this grass gives little pasture during that season, but when the water supply is sufficient and properly distributed it yields abundantly. Upon the ranch of Mr. Wheeler, at Reno, Nev., there are several pastures of bluegrass and white clover which by means of irrigation are kept in good condition through the season. In some localities it is considered a pest on account of its tendency to drive out other grasses where the conditions are favorable for the growth of bluegrass. Mr. G. F. Chapman, of Evanston, Wyo., a prominent ranchman, states that it forms a thin, low mat which can not be utilized for hay, and is not as valuable for pasture as other grasses. This is usually true when the land is not irrigated, as it tends to dry up during dry periods to a greater degree than native grasses, but it starts early in the spring and remains green well into the fall.

ORCHARD GRASS (*Dactylis glomerata.*)—This well-known grass should be grown much more extensively than it is. It resists drought better than most of the tame grasses grown in the East, and can be used for pasture or hay. On account of the tendency to grow in bunches when sown alone, it is best, especially for meadow, to sow with some other grass. For this purpose meadow fescue is well adapted. The latter occupies the spaces between the bunches of orchard grass and thus forms a more even and continuous surface for the mower. Both bloom at about the same time, and both are capable of resisting drought to about the same extent.

CHEAT (*Bromus secalinus*).—In the eastern United States this grass is known as a bad weed in grain fields, but in the Willamette Valley of western Oregon it is used quite extensively for hay. It is common to see cheat sown along the draws or other low portions of grain fields. Mr. T. H. Cooper, a farmer near Corvallis who utilizes cheat in this way, sows the seed broadcast in the fall at the rate of 1 to 1½ bushels per acre. He cuts the hay when it is in the dough state, which is about the last of June. The yield of seed is about 40 bushels per acre, a bushel weighing 35 to 40 pounds. It is quite probable that cheat could be used for forage in other localities.

PERENNIAL RYE GRASS (*Lolium perenne*).—This is commonly grown in the Willamette Valley and in some other parts of Oregon and Washington and proves to be a good grass for pasture and hay. Although not considered as a grass for dry regions, the trials at the experiment stations of Kansas, Colorado, and Wyoming indicate that it stands well as a drought-resisting grass. The variety known as Italian rye grass scarcely differs from this, except in usually having the chaff or flowering glume provided with a bristle at the tip, and in growing somewhat taller.

RAPE (*Brassica napus*).—A plant to be recommended for pasture in the cooler parts of the Northwest is rape. It is now used to a limited extent in several localities, especially in the Rocky Mountain region. As a forage plant for sheep and as succulent forage for summer and fall, rape is to be highly recommended. It is not easily injured by frost and hence is available as fall feed. The seed should be sown in June or July, and rape may consequently be grown as a catch crop after grain or other early maturing crops. Where there is sufficient moisture the seed may be sown broadcast, but in the drier regions much better results are obtained by sowing in drills far enough apart to permit of cultivation. In eight to ten weeks from sowing it is ready for use, and sheep can be turned into the field to pasture off the succulent growth. It is also an excellent feed for cattle, but they are likely to waste more by trampling than smaller stock.

FIELD PEAS (*Pisum arvense*).—This leguminous plant is adapted for use as a forage plant in the northern portion of the Northwest and farther south in the mountains. At present it seems to be grown to a comparatively limited extent, but it is worthy of culture to a much greater degree. Canada field peas can scarcely compete with alfalfa in the regions where the latter can be grown; but where alfalfa is not successful on account of the cooler climate the peas are an excellent substitute, in that they are rich in protein, and hence have a high feeding value. It is best to sow them with grain—oats, wheat, or barley being used for the combination—at the rate of 1 to 1½ bushels of peas to an equal quantity of grain. The crop can be cut for hay or used for pasture.

VETCHES.—In the Willamette Valley, Oregon, spring vetch (*Vicia sativa*) is commonly grown for hay and annual pasture. Mr. T. H. Cooper, of Corvallis, uses vetch for his silo, after which he uses green corn. He sows the seed in the fall with wheat or oats, 2 bushels of the mixture containing about a peck of grain. The crop is cut in June. Spring vetch is cultivated here and there in the cooler parts of the Northwest, but the crop as a whole is very insignificant when compared with the staple forage crops of the region. The plant is a legume, and can gather nitrogen from the air in a manner similar to clover and alfalfa. Hence it furnishes forage rich in protein and at the same time acts as a soil renovator. While spring vetch can not. be successfully grown over much of the area under consideration on account of the heat and drought, yet it is to be highly recommended for those localities having a cool, moist growing season. In the upper coast region it can be sown in the fall. In the mountain regions it should be sown in spring. It is best to sow with grain, as the latter tends to hold the vetch upright, and it can thus be handled for hay more easily, and also because the grain mixture produces a more evenly balanced feed. After the mixture of grain and vetch is cut, a second crop of vetch will usually appear, which can be saved for seed.

Hairy or sand vetch[a] (*Vicia villosa*) has been tried to a limited extent, but the results over most of the region described are not promising. It thrives, however, in the Palouse region and tends to become a weed in wheat fields.

BALING HAY.

As in other parts of the United States, it is customary to bale hay for convenience in transportation. Most of the hay consumed in the larger cities is of this kind. The baled hay upon the markets of the Northwest is for the most part restricted to alfalfa, clover, timothy, grain, and wild or native hay. In San Francisco and other cities of California, grain hay takes the lead, while at Seattle and the cities of the Sound, timothy is most used, the kind depending in part on the availability and in part on the demand of the market. Alfalfa is, in many cases, as available as timothy, or more so; but the latter is used in the cities in preference because it is believed to be more suitable for horses. In fact, timothy hay is taken as the standard upon the city markets. The type of press used at San Jose, Cal., is shown in Pl. VII, fig. 1.

The item of freight often enters greatly into the market price of baled hay. For example, during the summer of 1901, grain hay was worth $8 per ton at Raymond, a town upon the railroad, while at Yosemite the freight charges brought it up to $40 per ton, and at the same time the

---

[a] For further information upon the vetches, see Circular No. 6, Division of Agrostology, U. S. Dept. of Agriculture, "The Cultivated Vetches."

price of hay at Nome, in Alaska, was 7 cents per pound, even when double compressed.

Baled hay for export to Alaska, Hawaii, the Philippines, and other trans-oceanic points is compressed by the process known as "double compression." By means of powerful machines operated by electricity or hydraulic power, the hay, obtained by loosening ordinary baled hay, is compressed into square or cylindrical packages smaller and more compact than the ordinary bale. The hydraulic presses used for making the so-called round bales are similar to those used for making the cylindrical bales of cotton. The measurements of the different types of double-compressed bales are about as follows:

Ordinary square bale, 15 by 18 by 38 inches; weight, 160 pounds.

Square bale for Alaskan trade, 14 by 18 by 26 inches; weight, 100 pounds.

Round bale, 2 feet in diameter, 24 inches long; weight, 145 pounds, or 36 inches long, weight, 260 pounds.

The saving of space in transit may best be understood by comparing the weight and cubic contents of baled and compressed hay. The ordinary baled hay occupies 140 to 160 cubic feet per ton; the square double-compressed, 85 feet per ton; the round bales, 55 feet per ton.

The hay used for this process is almost exclusively timothy. The firm of Lilly, Bogardus & Company, Seattle, Wash., from whom much of the information concerning double-compressed bales was obtained, states that the timothy from the Ellensburg district, Wash., is much preferred on account of the fresh green color. A good quality is also obtained from the Spokane and Cœur d'Alene districts. On account of the damp weather, timothy from west Washington is not so satisfactory in appearance. There is some demand for clover hay in Alaska, and much grain hay is shipped to Honolulu. There is also a small but increasing demand for alfalfa bay for export.

DESCRIPTION OF PLATES.

PLATE I. Fig. 1.—Mast and boom stacker, with six-tined Jackson fork. The mast is held in place by guy ropes from the top. Leading to the right may be seen the rope to which is attached a team of horses. The base of the derrick is in the form of sled runners, so that the whole may be drawn along the stack by attaching a team. Fig. 2.—A cable derrick, provided with a grapple fork. The cable is supported by poles at the ends, and these in turn by guy ropes.

PLATE II. Fig. 1.—A derrick stacker, with six-tined Jackson or California fork. The derrick is substantial, and guy ropes are not necessary. Stakes driven into the ground around the base hold the derrick in place. Fig. 2.—The same derrick, showing details. It will be observed that from the peculiar attachment of the ropes, the hay is swung over the stack while it is being lifted from the wagon.

PLATE III. Types of derrick stackers. Fig. 1.—Derrick built on wheels and symmetrically braced. Fig. 2.—Derrick with revolving pole. In both forms the central pole rotates in sockets. The ropes are not attached to this derrick.

PLATE IV. Fig. 1.—A common type of hayrack. Fig. 2.—A pole stacker, with four-tined Jackson fork. The angle of the pole is regulated by a short beam. This is often replaced by a chain or rope. The derrick leans toward the stack sufficiently to swing the fork load of hay into position, when it is elevated.

PLATE V.—Types of racks in common use for feeding alfalfa to cattle. Fig. 1.—Lattice rack. Fig. 2.—Box rack.

PLATE VI.—Types of racks for feeding alfalfa to sheep. These racks are longer than those intended for cattle. Fig. 1.—Lattice rack. Fig. 2.—Box rack.

PLATE VII. Fig. 1.—Hay press, for baling grain hay, San José, Cal. Five men and three horses are employed; one man and horse drag the hay from the stack to the baler, with a four-tined Jackson fork; one man drives a team attached to the horse-power; two men pitch the hay into the baler; one man works the press and weighs the bales. Average time, three minutes to the bale. Weight of bales, about 210 pounds. Bales tied with rope. Fig. 2.—Field of brome grass at the Kansas Experiment Station, Manhattan, Kans. A seven-year-old boy stands in the grass.

28

O

FIG. 1.—MAST AND BOOM STACKER, WITH JACKSON FORK.

FIG. 2.—CABLE DERRICK, WITH GRAPPLE FORK.

FIG. 1.—DERRICK STACKER, WITH JACKSON FORK.

FIG. 2 —DERRICK STACKER, SHOWING DETAILS.

FIG. 1.—DERRICK MOUNTED ON WHEELS.

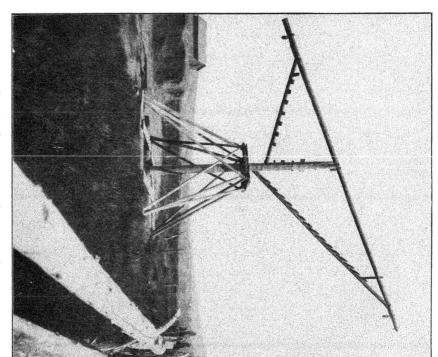

FIG. 2.—DERRICK WITH REVOLVING POLE.

FIG. 1.—A COMMON TYPE OF HAYRACK.

FIG. 2.—POLE STACKER, WITH JACKSON FORK.

Bul. 31, Bureau of Plant Industry, U. S. Dept. of Agriculture.

PLATE V.

FIG. 1.—LATTICE RACK FOR FEEDING ALFALFA TO CATTLE.

FIG. 2.—BOX RACK FOR FEEDING ALFALFA TO CATTLE.

Bul. 31, Bureau of Plant Industry, U. S. Dept. of Agriculture.

PLATE VI.

FIG. 1.—LATTICE RACK FOR FEEDING ALFALFA TO SHEEP.

FIG. 2.—BOX RACK FOR FEEDING ALFALFA TO SHEEP.

Lightning Source UK Ltd.
Milton Keynes UK
UKHW020629060119
334855UK00006B/220/P